NIGHT JOURNEY

NIGHT JOURNEY

poems by
Richard Widerkehr

SHANTI ARTS PUBLISHING
BRUNSWICK, MAINE

NIGHT JOURNEY

Copyright © 2022 Richard Widerkehr

All Rights Reserved
No part of this document may be reproduced or transmitted in any form or by any means without prior written permission of the publisher, except in the case of brief quotations embodied in critical reviews.

Published by Shanti Arts Publishing
Designed by Shanti Arts Designs

Cover image by Ria Harboe, *Walk with Me*.
Used with permission of the artist.

Shanti Arts LLC
193 Hillside Road
Brunswick, Maine 04011
shantiarts.com

Printed in the United States of America

The poems about patients on 4-South are fictional, and 4-South is a fictional place. In the poem "Elegy in a Costco Lot," the words "her chewy heart" are by Terrence Hayes.

ISBN: 978-1-956056-38-9 (softcover)

Library of Congress Control Number: 2022937348

for Linda, again

Contents

Her Story of Fire

Where the Voices Took Her	13
Looking for My Sister	14
Her Story of Fire	15
Afterward	28
We've Come to Moclips to Forget	30

The Possum on Irving Street

Green's Idea	45
At the Alger Swap Meet	46
Now the Lion Sun	48
Feeding the Animals	49
Clarity	50
Her Peonies	51
Elegy in a Costco Lot	52
At O'Hare Airport: Her Foxgloves	53
Early Sunday Morning during Threats of War with North Korea	54
Another Shooter	55
The Possum on Irving Street after Evening Services	56
Homage to Raoul Wallenburg	57
"Devereux"	58
When We Send My Sister Birkenstocks, She Gives Them Away	60
Missing	61
As We Drive South through Skagit Valley near Midnight	62
Taking Him Home	63
In a Lutheran Cemetery in Seattle	64
Before the Party, You Tell Me, I've Got Three Years Left, Maybe Five	65

Someone Else's Life

Sidewalks and My Sister	69
Almost Every Crevice: A Counselor on 4-South Speaks	70
Balefire, Says Chloe on Her Borrowed Phone	71

Late Afternoon in August: 1970	72
Did You Ever Call the Cops on Me?	
Asks My Sister on the Phone	73
We Visit the Muscatels near Christmas	74
Almost Dawn near Squalicum Lake	75
What Happened	76
Prophet on Railroad Avenue	77
As We Get Ready to Go See Chloe	78
Wildfires, St. Paul Riots	79
The Whale Thank-You Card You Send Me	
from the Museum of Natural History	80
Kristallnacht, 1938: Night of Shattered Glass	81
At Twilight near Agate Bay	82
Baby Evening Grosbeak Caught in Blueberry Netting	83
No Palaces, No Bees	84
This Wind	86
After Sunup Near the Y Road	87
Deer in Fog at Twilight near Squalicum Lake Road	88
Night Journey	89
Aubade: As We Stand under the Eleventh Street Bridge	90
Acknowledgments	93
About the Author	95

In a dark time, the eye begins to see.
—Theodore Roethke

ONE

Her Story of Fire

Where the Voices Took Her

Where the air people
build their flowery cities; where llamas
don't have nasty habits but stare
out of their dark eyes;
where Shangri-La falls away in snowfields
and she slides down the white slopes,
and the planet's radioactive waste
can't seep through the snow;
where ghost dancers
resurrect the dreaming herds
whose white clouds block the sun;
where everyone's ears are ringing with a hum
like a TV's turned down low;
where lovers get married on mountaintops,
wearing T-shirts, shorts, sunglasses,
and long, dark preacher coats—
they drink champagne and climb a sheer rock face
as the sun comes out and the hidden lakes
lie scraped of all their pain.

Someday I'll cross her frozen fields,
climbing gear dangling from my neck.
I'll squeeze the needled
sunlight in my fist and walk through
her stampeding clouds, her avalanche of sighs.
Come back, come back.

Looking for My Sister

My father and I hunt in the darkness
for Chloe who sleeps in her van.
I once thought he created
this city, walking into it each morning,
hauling it back each night,
so Chloe and I could clog the drains
on Grandma's terrace,
floating our toy ships. Now in the darkness,
sweat falls from my father's eyes
as we trudge by men offering to rinse
our misty eyeglasses, holding their rags out
to be kissed.   Here she is, lying between
two buildings, under a piece of corrugated tin
slanting from one wall to another. We stare
at her light breathing, her tightly-closed eyes.
My God, she's got her *sleepy-top*,
that tattered, old pajama top she wrapped
around the thumb. Somewhere a black wing
tears into the sky the way a flock
of dunlins turns from white to black. But here
the sky goes blue-black, black, blue-black,
and we can't see her.

Her Story of Fire

1

I'm a psychic detective,
sings Chloe,
as she walks down Elm Street
toward dawn,

praying over the roofs
of dark houses,
refusing
to answer questions.

Is she taking her meds?
Did she smash
our mom's hummingbird
feeder?

Addressed in music,
Chloe can only
keep going, hiding her face
from the sun

as it presses
against the walls of dark gardens,
and the sea, being a sea,
says nothing.

2

She says, *You whom I pray for,*
you don't know I exist—
my meds were gazebos,
they didn't work.

The roofs of your houses
know me.
The sun, my favorite sister,
never sleeps.

The walls of dark gardens—
shawls for my arms.
And yes, the sea says nothing,
but we rest.

3

Last night, Chloe, I dreamt
you cried out to me,
It's a hospital, not a hospice!
Tall as a flower, you stood on a stage.

I was down in a pit,
huddled with so many others,
men holding out their rags,
their cut wrists.

A scent of pine needles....
And yet we lived,
someone shouted, and stars
called out your name.

4

She says, *I don't believe
in hospitals. There were too many
dead-swan poets there,
reading their swanny poems.*

*See the wind
flying over the white city.
The stars
open their dark arms.*

*The dead, they don't forget us.
I'm not up on a stage.
You're not down
in a crowd.*

5

I've looked for you in cities,
where the walls,
where the night, where your van . . .
In tent camps

where clouds of gulls wheeled in
from the sea,
flying like whitecaps, saying,
What's next?

By the expressway ramp
with its shiny, white steps,
by railroad tracks where the Scotch broom
whispered, *Yes.*

By Fuehrey's Machine Shop,
in a gully
sculpted of dust,
where we raced our toy cars,

where a sultan's palace
crumbled,
where sand in the sandbox
nestled in clefts.

6

The rain
flies up from the sea.
A jealous god,
it will have no other gods.

Why do you
do it? You can't argue
with the sea.
It does what a sea does.

Me, I smashed nothing.
I didn't cause the suffering
of our mother. In whose dark arms
did you lie?

7

Where cliffs of rain
can't rest, where the sea's
tug and thrust,
where its obsessive eddies

take away my breath.
Where you chased a bag of cellophane
down a windy beach.
Past bleached logs,

past the muddy slough—
with its stream
of cobalt
and dark, coppery amber.

Past a lump of Styrofoam
big as a sea chest.
A lunkhead's escutcheon,
you said.

Where the footbridge swayed,
where we threw dirt-clods,
where your wind harp
was sky blue.

8

A thin box whose wires
the wind strays over...
At night, at work,
I sit in a waiting room,

listening to a stranger
muttering, *Death, death*—
he's unsure
he wants to be admitted.

We sign and counter-sign
the Voluntary form,
and then
we climb the stairs.

When I knew you, Chloe,
we were unformed.
You were a leaf, sunlit,
the quick air that plays over fire,

surviving as music, or memory,
which the wind gives back.
My ribs, your wrists,
this wind, that lyre.

9

Sometimes, says Chloe,
I have a bad hair day.
My hands curl like claws.
My eyes, a fixed stare.

If I get mad
when Mom brings food,
don't ask why—
that's how it is.

Don't ask how a scar
becomes the night sky—
how a harp
is my sweet jail.

How my ribcage,
bits of mist—
how the roofs of a town
tell the story of fire.

10

On the freeway,
you floored the Bonneville,
the Beach Boys'
"Fun, fun, fun" on the radio.

Give them the finger,
you said.
If much remains nameless,
much remains.

A smoky skyline,
runnels in dust.
By the lake, a nurse-log
sword ferns jut from.

11

After such music,
after the wires were tied
to my wrists,
don't ask why.

After the rain, the garden
with eggshell compost,
the water
we had to boil.

After the mountain
was clearcut. After the sky's
white light, its eyes
of peacock blue,

*after the walls crumbled
and the cliffs rose up.
Tell no one,
not even the rain.*

*After such music,
silence is right.
Fire is a fierce angel.
Fire is right.*

12

Chloe, when I went
to your ward, you said the wires
to your bed
held your thoughts.

That firelight
is your quiet lake,
and compost
is the opposite of desire.

That the old man
on the mountain has a beard
that smells
like sardines. That he likes

to hear himself talk.
That he stalks.
That at night he crawls
out of the sea. That he lies.

That you punched
off his glasses, that the walls
of your quiet room
have eyes.

That I shouldn't come here,
not ever.
That I look like him, ta-ta,
toodle-oo.

13

You sound like him, too.
Like the sea.
Are you sure you're not
the sea?

Me, I loved fire,
lightning, I-5, and what else?
No,
nothing else.

14

I've seen how
your hands curl up, heard how
Mom clips your nails,
how you wear a ragged hood.

Barefoot, by the lake,
we scuffed pine needles...
The sky was our sky.
Now you tug Mom's arm

from the steering wheel
and shout, *No!*
if she drives
down the wrong street.

15

Our small lake
was a myth.
Do the freaking math,
stupid.

Me, I ate clouds and dirt.
You built your separate bridge.
Look, you can't ever
say the sea, or pay lip service.

I tug her arm
'cause she's a nitwit.
When a street's the wrong color,
that changes everything.

16

Dark Elm Street
by the freeway, isn't a fjord
to the sun.
By the underpass, I've waited.

On a ward
of domes and eyes,
I look for you. I carry
my set of keys.

I sing "In My Life"
or "Me and Bobbie McGee."
In the solarium,
I listen.

Something left to lose...
Are you
protecting someone, Chloe?
From the sea's

bitter shoals and reefs,
its history,
its need to be told
it's the sea.

17

You can't see me,
yet I protect you.
By leaving
I stay with you.

Stars with their dark coats...
The night has many arms.
Each day, a bridge sways over.
A wind shines.

No, there are no ashes.
You can't
seal them in a tree.
It's too hard.

As in memory
I become something else,
so your longing can't be my rescue.
My pain isn't your pain.

Afterward

1

She's been out there all night in the snow.
The swing is her childhood swing.
When we ask if she's going to do that all night,
she says, *That's the general idea.*
We go out with trays of steaming mugs
and TV dinners. She says the meat
costs twenty dollars a pound. She doesn't
eat meat. We offer quilts, books, lawn chairs,
framed certificates from forty years ago.
She goes on swinging. The snow
keeps falling. She says there's a man
in the house with a butcher's knife who last night
asked her to make her mark on his blade.
She says she told him her initials.

2

Now the snow's stopped falling,
fields and roofs and branches thickly laden—
froth blown from the fir trees
goes like an afterthought.
I can't tell if the silence
is a survivor's stubborn gaze
or mute astonishment. There was gaiety
and something else.
All day I've gone through letters
from twenty years ago, before
the voices took you. You wrote me
from Niagara Falls—*an ocean
stood on end*, you said,
no before or after.

We've Come to Moclips to Forget

1

How you wear a ragged hood, how you've stopped answering
the phone because you think it's bugged,

how you walk six miles barefoot to your bank,
how you can't be detained, no danger to self or others.

Who's after her? our mother asked.
What could she have done?

Linda and I, we've come to this cold stream on the coast,
where ghost trees crash and snag in winter storms,

driven upstream to a gravel shoal where thick leaves
of sedum sprout, deep in summer.

An upturned stump, stuck headfirst in the gravel,
gray-and-black root system snarled in the air—
a geological prank, miscreant ghost wave?

Yesterday, we called your motel:
We have no one here by that name.
Lately, I can't pray.

2

We pick our way on a trail of encroaching
salal, primroses, blackberries—away from the sea
with its burning wind, its distances, its long, low breakers

shushing and crashing, as if hugging themselves, hoarding
    their ammunition,
as ripples lapped at our toes.

In the woods by a flat, black stream,
hundred-year-old fir trees, lower limbs lopped off,
stubs jutting out.

Two fallen trees nearly dam the stream,
branches bleached dead-white.

One skeleton tree with a double trunk,
the black stream reflecting nothing.

We don't know your diagnosis, but my father once said,
If she's not schizophrenic, I'm a lamp-post!

This is no *vale of soul-making*. I see no reason
these trees were put here, stripped naked—
just nature with its storms, genetic engines, and disease.

Can these bones live? God asked the prophet.
Only Thou knowest, Ezekiel replied.

3

*Hey, you know nothing, nada, my brother, and that's how I want it.
I keep you far, I keep you near. Toodle-oo.*

When the mountain stops being a mountain,
and it will,
when the desert stops being a desert,
and it will,

when the sun is torn out of its socket,
and it will be...

There are streams so deep, no one should enter.

*Don't open that bottle with a message in it.
Leave it for the wind, the sun, and the crows.*

4

There's This Talk We Have

Me: *It should be easier to detain people.
She's never been tried on meds.*

Linda: *That's a slippery slope. Lots of people,
back in the fifties, got put away for years.*

*But she's scared to death. Lives like a hermit.
My mother thinks she gets food from the dumpster.*

*With Chloe's thing about organic food?
I don't think so.*

*Ok, I don't like where I'm going, but I want to trust
some philosopher king, wise enough to know*

*which ones are eccentric, and which ones,
their lives off meds are just so broken . . .*

*That's it. I don't trust anyone
to know. There have to be written laws.*

Christ, she's more Jewish than I am,
and maybe she's right,

or we're both looking at different sides
of the same green glass buoy.

5

I remember my sister's laugh, how it spilled out
in sunlight, how one summer

she ran after my friends and me, and we
ran away, because we could,

we were the older kids . . . Now her quavery voice
on the phone, each question insistent,

a quaking river, a sea that longs to be contained
in a glass of water.

6

Chloe Speaks—

I only want a glass of water, really clean water, not the crap from the tap, there must be some kind of filter I can get, I only want the sea to keep away, and you, too, bro, and you and you, too, amscray, scram, I only want some good organic basmati to eat, does Mom eat basmati, does she take vitamins, the really good stuff, not the cheap stuff, I mean Omega-3 and fish oil and fatty acids and really clean water, not polluted like in China, all those people in China, so many, all those people floating in the water, yes, in China, keep away, keep away, how far does Mom live from the water, just three miles, huh? I don't care if she's up on a hill, that's nothing, think of what happened, all those people, what's her doctor's name, is she getting good care, I mean you have to be careful, and the sea, it can creep up on you, or the tide, it can go out, and there's this gull picking at a fish, it's four-foot-long, thin like an eel, but it has a tail, see, and the thing flops over, and the gull keeps picking at its tail fins, all those people in China, not just China, and this wave comes in and picks them up, hey, don't tell me Byron says I look thin, I look the same, you sent him to spy on me, bullshit you didn't, like I believe you, right, he just saw me on Electric and stopped to say hello, put Mom on the phone...

7

You Have to Eat, Chloe—

Our mother's voice, soft from her stroke, yet what she says is so
perfect. I think how she took meals to Chloe all those years
till she was 90, till she had her stroke.

8

While I was on the train, on my way to see our mother,
she had been driving Chloe to her motel. I found Mom sitting at
her kitchen table, one side of her face fallen, her speech slurred.
She limped when she got up to kiss me hello. She told me her hand
had fallen from the steering wheel as she was driving Chloe,
and my sister said, *You may be having a stroke, Mom.*
Driving with one hand, Mom dropped her off, and Chloe
ran into her motel. *She just ran*, our mother said.

9

That's Bullshit—

What my sister says when I tell her our mother
could've gotten help, if she'd gotten to the hospital sooner.

10

What Chloe Doesn't Tell Me—

*Her hand, it just fell down from the wheel, but there were
all these people in China, I had to help them, I'm not God, I
can't be everywhere, and you were coming down, how was
I supposed to know your train would be two hours late, you
had to help her, I couldn't do it, but do you think I could take
care of her now? You don't think so? I mean, it's costing so
much money . . .*

11

My sister mails a package to our mother—
twelve bottles of vitamins.

12

Why Chloe Didn't Call 911—

Was she scared, our mother asks me,
of getting detained?

I believe there are certain temperatures
at which fire freezes,

and the green glass buoy you're left with
is the green glass buoy you're left with.

13

Green Glass Buoy—

I wash up at your feet—
gray-green, the size of a grapefruit,
smooth as a beach agate,

vitreous as moonstone—
translucent, not glowing,
holding what you can't know.

Japanese fishermen sent me
to your coast,
spinning free from their nets.

I know what the night does
when it can't sleep, how mountains
reach out, when they can't meet.

The sea has its needs.
Let the black waves
tumble me back under, set me afloat.

14

I stand at this threshold, doorsill.
The sea breathes in,
breathes out:

Green
glass buoy, green glass
buoy...

One crow, indignant, fixes its claw
on a broken sand dollar
and pecks it to bits.

15

America, we have all this money,
and we let our people sleep on the streets.

At least Chloe has a roof and food,
and if she read this, perhaps she'd say,

Don't chant your sad canticles
over me, brother mine.

16

Sister of *Don't send me anything.*
We send you checks, and you tear them up.

I know a man whose sister drops bottled water
and socks at the feet of the homeless.

I know a woman who's afraid to testify in court
or write an affidavit saying her husband cuts on himself.

I know a man who doesn't know where his son is.
He asks if my sister is safe. I say, *We think so.*

I've taken phone calls from people across the country,
asking if we have their daughter in our hospital,

and unless the patient has signed a piece of paper,
I'm supposed to say, *I can neither affirm nor deny*

the presence . . . One man called, convinced
his son was on our unit. I went out on a limb,

told him he wasn't. *Bullshit!* he said. *I'll search
every hell hole on the west coast till I find him.*

17

I can neither affirm nor deny the presence
of God's mercy,

can neither affirm nor deny that smoke doesn't pour
back down into black chimneys,

that night isn't so in love with sunlight
that it blinds itself in hope of mercy's pale gray dawn.

18

I've seen hands, self-mutilated,
the blood flow almost cut off, the flesh

a piece of swollen, gray gauze.
I've seen arterial blood spurt from a woman's wrist

when she yanked out the tubes of her dialysis machine.
I've seen a man, more than one man, bang his head

against our walls, so we had to restrain him.
Do you see this, God? Or have your eyes

gotten tired from taking them out each night,
putting them in each day? Or have you

secretly been keeping my sister as well
as she can be? Since absence must bring us together.

19

Chloe Borrows a Phone Card

When the ocean turns into a forest floor, bro,
maybe we'll meet.

When the desert gives up its sapphires and gila monsters?
When the rain is an angel that takes us into its house?

When sleep is black rain that kisses the half-closed eyelids
of someone's sister, father, mother,
and we can say, *They're treated well, and with kindness.*

Brother mine, I'm not sick. Please don't worry.
Don't you see, we're all blessed?

TWO

The Possum on Irving Street

Green's Idea

My window's filled with birch leaves this morning—
green's idea of being sunlit. No darning needles
back and forth patrolling, just this sheen

of green flame singeing no one. Glasses off,
my world's all leaves—mosaics, soft points,
thawing pieces in blurred air. The branches,

switches waved by five-year-olds
in speckled walls, in sunspots—
the spaces between leaves: shadows.

At the Alger Swap Meet

—for P. H.

I see your name in a fifteen-year-old *Poetry* magazine,
past the socket wrenches and boxes
of nuts and bolts—
for five bucks, an *Encyclopedia Britannica*
missing volumes A through G. The owner's daughter
is telling her father about her sewing
and computer classes. He sits, feet propped
on the counter by the register
under a six-foot-high, yellow-and-green stuffed dog
with pitiful eyes.
      Your lines
evoke the purity of deserts.

I'm so happy to find your poem,
though it's been almost twenty-five years
since I read you in the Hopwood Room
in Ann Arbor...all around me glass cases
of prize-winning manuscripts,
tables of little magazines, the green inner room
where a gruff scholar and writer waited,
and now since I've brought up Michigan,
I've got to mention summer and an open window,
please forgive me, and one house light
shining in the valley
below....
      I glare at
the goddamn, pitiful, stuffed dog,
patron saint of Putting in Too Much—
chain saws, electric typewriters, pots and pans,

a road narrowing into dark trees at twilight
near the Sleeping Bear Dunes
where we never met and where the missing volumes
lie mercifully open,
since obscurity has its uses, God knows,
on the outskirts of Alger, Washington,
on Highway 99.

Now the Lion Sun

—April 2020

For a while, I've wanted to say the word *disquiet*.

As we self-quarantine, and the pharmacy techs,
the grocery checkers go to work,
we sip coffee from our royal-blue cups.

Fir branches in shadow at the edge
of our field make a human figure, arms upraised.
Yesterday, I saw this photo of a lion.

In that zoo with no bars, it lifted its head,
as if toward harsh savannas, sun-struck grass.
Since she saw clients exposed to the virus,

Linda has stayed home—no signs of fever,
no weakening armies of breath.
Now the lion sun.

On the edges of dark, naked alders—
the moss on our goat shed glows.

Feeding the Animals

Staring out the window
at the apple trees just
coming into bloom—woodsmoke
drifting through wet branches,
the small, white blossoms
more like bits of Kleenex
than blossoms—
I'm warm as the wood stove
cranks itself up, and the rain
seems almost theoretical.

When I go out,
the high, straight tops
of fir trees deep
inside themselves sway slightly.
The ducks poke and slurp
in mud. The goats
baa in their shed
like wind-up plastic dolls.
I give them grain,
put out mash for the ducks.
I'm swathed in wool
and latex, my face
and hands wet; the rest
of me is warm.

Clarity

Trees, hills, foghorns—the dank air
had filled them, sifting in
without my noticing. And now
yellow headlights, blue fields, and hills
thinned to an airy consistency
weren't real. Couldn't the world
be itself? Did it need intimate
hints and mysteries? Couldn't trees
be trees, stubborn and quiet, and hills
sit up the way they do at twilight,
about to pounce?

Her Peonies

—for L.

They have opened their folded wings,
whorls of white linen.
There's no wind.
Bees hover like fat battle-stars,
totter in spasms, suckle at the tips
of stamens, dive into the petals,
butt at the slow explosions.

The red, swollen buds—
no, the bees must not touch them.
They'll open when it's time.
It's July, and the sun, a dying monarch,
burnishes each ember.
Though it's cold and clouds
enfold us, shadows almost glow
inside white petals.

Elegy in a Costco Lot

—in memory of S.O. and C.C.

By tin warehouses, a sheath of gold-yellow
in the sky; an overhang of gaunt gray.
People line up for foodstuffs.
Early this morning, I saw a photo
of an art installation—orange wedges,
wire, nails, an LED lightbulb.

A science experiment for Susan's fourth-graders?
Last July when her doctor said *hospice*,
she faced the wall, no longer spooned in
Linda's homemade corn chowder. For a week,
we watched her choke, cough. She stopped
the clinical trial. Oxygen tubes not enough
oxygen; the nurse upped her morphine.

This sky has paled to a clear ether
like back then. Not enough speed
in the light for God's anorexic angel
to lift its grievous wings? *Her chewy heart.*
Words from last summer. *After the first death,
there is no other?* No, there's another.

At O'Hare Airport: Her Foxgloves

As I walk toward baggage check, my cell phone rings.
In an urgent, neutral tone, the male nurse
says, *The retest confirms it—your PSA has doubled.*
He suggests an appointment with oncology.
I sit on a steel bench. As passengers

glide toward terminals, I picture our mother's garden
where we sang, walk toward glass walls,
then see I've forgotten my briefcase
and turn back. Amazing, still there.
I get on the moving walkway,

find a taxi driven by a young man from Ethiopia,
ask what his country is like. We ride
into the city, lights flashing, buildings floating.
He punches a number on his cell phone,
tilts the screen toward me.

I watch a video about caverns—
white rubble, stone burrows curving
in sunlight. *King Solomon went there*,
the driver tells me. *I'm Jewish*,
I say. *Yisrael*, he says, exactly

as we pronounce it in synagogue.
I can't picture our mother's foxgloves—
spots of magenta ink in crevices,
upturned bells. His smile
goes back three thousand years.

Early Sunday Morning during Threats of War with North Korea

As we listen to brown squirrels tousle with the Steller's jays
  outside this window, our quiet breathing isn't warm bread
in a basket. As we lie in each other's arms, you touch my hand

and say, *Don't worry.* Outside our red house, pale stars
  that woke soldiers at dawn in another country... In the nests
in naked alders, jays screech, seem to have the last say.

Another Shooter

When the pale sky lets in a chink of light over the rim
of the foothills, we can't help glancing at the sun.
Last night's news tasted like salt. Still half-asleep,
we wait, as if for a brand-new diaspora,

a city with bread and honey. As the coffee maker
brews our coffee, and the sun gets round,
more golden, we touch each other, almost afraid.
Sun like a wind, scattered from the edge

of a nebula. After two cups of coffee,
I read how police traced our latest murderer
to the Red Roof Inn near Round Rock, Texas.

How strange, to stand as witnesses this morning.
Our phone rings, numbers flash on a screen. *Not in use,*
says the display. The sun, this blinding gift.

The Possum on Irving Street after Evening Services

—written the week of the Douglas High School shootings

Under this streetlight, a possum lopes by brick houses,
its gray-white muzzle and needle nose
low to the street.

Take action, said our rabbi. *Write letters.*

Standing by my car, I wonder
who needs a bump stock
for self-defense.

Not right or wrong, needing no carry permit,
the possum skitters into an alley.

The empty street, the streetlight—

an alertness sends out tendrils,
almost part of the dark.

Homage to Raoul Wallenburg

When the last devouring wave swept Hungary's Jews
toward the death camps near the end of that war,
he boarded trains, bribed Nazis, provided passports,
saved thousands from the crematoriums.
If his courage had been visible, what color
might that be, a Steller's jay blue-black at night?
Disguised, but not enough to joke with them
as cattle cars passed certain chimneys,
a scent not smoke, not creosote.

"Devereux"

—letter to E.

When I read that poem where your mother-in-law said,
    You've always
been a little Jew about the waist, I think of my Grandpa and Baba
on Coney Island—clotheslines, smell of asphalt in the heat.

They spoke Yiddish. No, I didn't think *we* yet; my sister
and I didn't want to be *too Jewish*. The mannequins
in Grandpa's office fixtures shop on Broome Street,

Lower East Side. *Fuh-GET-about-it,* said my cousin
Judy, who built her mansion in Jersey with breezeways.
What a word. *Breezeway.* In college, I used a pen name,

Devereux, a cigarette man on a black op, noble, a bit dishabille,
half-hidden like sun in smoke from wildfires on the hills.
When I read Nietzsche, my father said, *The Nazis*

got a lot from him, like your mom's mother, that anti-Semite…
My mom converted to keep the peace
but said, *It was the stupidest thing I ever did. On a hot day*

in July, I walked uphill and converted. He said Baba and Grandpa
would sit shiva if I didn't. Years later, he told me
that never would've happened.

Yes, something burning, this cargo of coal smoldering.
It was all a dance, said Judy, a fire dancer on no meds
who went down in her own mentally ill-lit flames.

Like you, she had a coat of no opprobrium
she performed in. At age 65, I got my adult Bar Mitzvah.
My 95-year-old mother said, *Remember,*

you're half-Christian. I said nothing, Erin.

When We Send My Sister Birkenstocks, She Gives Them Away

Outside the window of our small red house,
this strand of spider web in the wind. *I can't spare
the least insect or angel*, said Chloe. She spares
angels, squashes bugs? My sister no longer

hears voices, still wears her ragged hood.
She has her own place now; she's safe.
Between a dark fir tree and our new deck,
this filament sways in the sun. As if a weaver's

shuttle, unseen, strove back and forth
across it, the thread glistens. *Don't worry,
bro,* she said. *I pray over least signs like this.*

*They don't mark a spider's teahouse;
they're not a sultan's palace in the sun.*

Two dragonflies shine, disappear.

Missing

—Lake Padden, Rosh Hashanah

My sister sleeps with the moon in her cardboard box.
Force her to take meds, says Linda, *and she'll run.*
We've tossed crusts to mallards, Khaki Campbells,
wished each other a good year—now a poster

of the missing girl, her portrait on this phone pole,
her name, her age, father's number, another
for the police, a case number. A random wind
picks up red maple leaves, swirls them over our path.

As We Drive South through Skagit Valley near Midnight

Across black fields, the urns of house lights—
my hands on the wheel, our car in the dark,
nothing on the radio. The fields
slide by, not my father's.

The night, a well, fills almost every slat,
each sway-back barn gone slack.
The farthest lights, his stories...
I hug the wheel, squint hard.

Taking Him Home

    —letter to L.E.

There's this fact, your dead father, his river,
which you happen to like—not so much the snow,
except for the way it hasn't turned
to freezing rain. There's the radio tower
that can't amp up your slightly-crackly voice.
It isn't boring being a voice, but nothing
can make you describe that train ride
with his plummy gray casket.
                              I'm cold,
he says, touching the sleeve of your coat.
Please, don't get up, you call out.
Oh-oh, will you need a diction of sobs
and whistle stops to tell this? His footsteps,
your steps, the black stream in his field.
No, your coat isn't broadcloth; it's worsted,
you tell him. *Worsted*, what a word.
Snow on the inside of your wrist—
do you give him the coat? *All the doors
are open,* he says, *no endings that I know.*

In a Lutheran Cemetery in Seattle

No flying horses lift their wings in the sun. A black-crested
   night heron has crept from its pool. My mother rests
in no grave, sleeps in no garden. On our mahogany gate-leg

table she left us, her urn rests beneath two stylized herons.
   Don't pull such a grave face, she might say. *We have
the Texaco station, the flying red horse on Woodhaven.*

In my Mom's story of gardens, nine spotted ladybugs
   on a foxglove bell one June. "What Is So Rare
As A Day In June?" Her favorite poem.

Sugarloaf was my best garden, she said. Chopped-back
   roses on Wood Road. Her death, a hanging garden
near the sun. Now a bee with gold on its thighs

in this rock garden, beside the graves of twelve reverend
   mothers. Once, we counted twenty-seven herons.

Before the Party, You Tell Me, I've Got Three Years Left, Maybe Five

—for G.

We're hallelujah fruit pies, you said in your book.
In this luminous room, we play Scrabble with friends.
I'm solemn as a goldfish; a golem in a plastic baggie.

I try to picture mustard fields, bright water; in your book,
you quoted me, *All the doors are open, no endings
I know.* I said *that?* Sometimes, as we've gone over

each other's poems, I've thought there must be
this separate wind, one story. Some words in this game:
crow, sorrow. You say *meat bag.* That's two words,

I say. *Want to challenge me?* you ask. *Our bodies
are meat bags.* Here, these deep blue curtains,
an off-white carpet, lamplit walls.

Our souls are doors? No wind; it's night.
In your book, you said, *I'm window on water.*

THREE

Someone Else's Life

Sidewalks and My Sister

Our mother, thin and brittle, almost floats
from her hospital bed. When we were kids,
Chloe and I never stepped on cracks
in sidewalks, as if any fissure might spread.

At least she's safe, I tell our mother.
As I sit by this bed, I picture
my sister in her ragged hood,
her tattered cloak of breath.

Almost Every Crevice:
A Counselor on 4-South Speaks

On a certain morning as Izzy walks barefoot in the snow
  to get groceries, she falls and leaves the truthful streets
of her town. As she tumbles into cavernous halls and foyers,

voices inside tall chifforobes curse at her, and she yells, *Get away,*
  Puta. In our E.R. waiting room cops have brought her to,
three patients are upset. When the doc asks Izzy if she can see

how people have a problem with her yelling, Izzy says,
  Yeah, I see it. But if it isn't a problem for me, it shouldn't
be one for them. How our weekend doc, Ellie,

tries not to smile, and Izzy shouts, *Don't laugh at me.*
  Her eyes two gun turrets. *I'm not laughing at you,* says Ellie.
It's just I never thought of it that way. In her cool voice,

she gently asks, *Doesn't Puta mean whore in Spanish?*
  Izzy bows her head, weeps quietly. Next morning
on our unit, she accepts meds, I read her her rights,

and after five days she stops yelling. *I haven't stopped*
  falling in snow, she tells us, *but the voices aren't so bad.*
I want to ask my sister, *Can't you try meds*

as a crazy experiment? I picture her street, her steeple
  like a knitting needle, the houses shrouded for someone's
arrival, how the snow fills almost every crevice.

Balefire, Says Chloe on Her Borrowed Phone

*In my cardboard box,
the moon lives with me,
not vice versa.*

*He scours no tats,
no scratch marks
on his sinews,*

*may not scrape
together that field
of trucks and weeds*

*in the sun,
this balefire
eaten by bees . . .*

*He will not feast
his thirst ten times
mere marrow,*

*we eat no leaves,
no grass, bro—
toodle-oo.*

Late Afternoon in August: 1970

—after our grandmother's death

Under dusty elm leaves in the heat, we walk
to the train station—lawn sprinklers
back and forth in the sun.

We'll meet in mirrors, says my sister.
It's all possible. She means we come back
after death? Almost as if asleep,

the evening deepens on wide porches.
Dust and sunlight, half-deserted streets—
she hears no voices, doesn't yet call me *bro*.

Did You Ever Call the Cops on Me? Asks My Sister on the Phone

The sun has three hearts
says Chloe, *one for the wind,*
two for its dark arms.

Did you ever call
the cops on me, bro . . . ? No, I say,
but when she moved our

Mom out of her own
living room, away from her
Steinway, I wanted . . .

There's this bobcat in
the snow, I tell her—how cold,
hungry it must be.

Feels like I'm forcing
a whetstone to speak, she says.
Dilemmas and drums.

I'd like to see you,
I tell my sister—she says,
I look terrible.

We Visit the Muscatels near Christmas

Almost up to the ceiling, flowing to gray-green carpets—
all the angel hair tinsel on their tree. An icy halo shimmers
in the heat from radiators, the kind my sister bangs on

to tell Francine, *Come out and play.* Isinglass,
said Mrs. Tate at school. *Eyes in glass?*
I pictured fish bladders in Science class.

At our house it's still Hanukkah. *Don't tell Dad,*
says Chloe; we look at each other, the shroud of filaments,
the angels' hair... I take my sister's hand.

Almost Dawn near Squalicum Lake

—after Chloe gets her own place again

In the dark all I hear, this water lapping
at pilings, a stone's throw
from our house.

Perhaps, our mother has crossed over
to a street where the wind is a leaf,
that beggar on Railroad

in an alcove on her sleeping bag...
All the doors are open, said our father,
no endings I know.

What Happened

Someone I never knew but always knew
danced in our basement at her ballet barre
on polished hardwood floors. In her room,
she wondered why I argued with our father

who was always right, went on long walks
with him, till it was almost dark—
the force of combinations in his steps,
the weighted chess piece on stone tables

in the city park where I watched him
and the old men play. Our mother
at her Steinway drowned him out, and when
she threw her coffee cup at him,

we vowed we'd never be like them.
Her empty living room, our staircase,
the window seat, the leaded windows—
if anyone knew best, she never said,

till winter with its lessons of deep snow,
the car left running, footsteps, arched elm trees,
the night sky, mercy slow as any stone...

When you heard voices, maybe they told you.

Prophet on Railroad Avenue

Her face reminds us of scorched trees, ash-gray, almost silver.
  Asphalt, tar, and rain, she shouts. *Gonna melt your cities--
haloes and eyes.* She's all the news we cannot want to hear.

A blast furnace in our basements, is she sent by a god,
  not done till she's done with us? I stuff three bucks
in her cup. *Here*, she says, *eat this seed.*

As We Get Ready to Go See Chloe

I'm packing clothes, folding laundry,
fumbling with last night's dreams—certain lamp
stands missing, someone's life at stake...

I used to float those mornings, almost awake,
over the chifforobe in our hallway, by the blond-oak
dining-room table we went round and round.

This ceiling with no shadows, no pencil marks
on foyer walls to measure our separate heights—
it isn't summer—no sounds from the street,

no light through the blinds. The silver
lamp stands, cloudless rooms—
this must be someone else's life.

Wildfires, St. Paul Riots

In August when fireweed turned white,
and the sun hung like a poppy in smoke—
Beauty takes a beating in the streets,
I wrote, *and truth tries to do too much.*

That night the orange half-moon,
a smudge pot in funerary shadows—
now my sister says, *There's no virus,
it's a plot by the government—*

*this host's an army, a throng.
Fumes and rumors fuse no sinews, bro.*
George Floyd is dead, I tell her.
And the sun has the gall to come up.

The Whale Thank-You Card You Send Me from the Museum of Natural History

We cannot know if my sister read or even opened
your letter I forwarded, cannot know if she remembers
the blue whale suspended from a wire in that atrium

tall as our school auditorium where Mrs. Logie read
us psalms about gates and thrones. The small black eye—
if Chloe still hears voices, wears a ragged hood,

listens to talk radio about living off the grid...
Things happen, bro, she says, *and we're not the same.*
Stars aren't stars; snow isn't snow.

Kristallnacht, 1938: Night of Shattered Glass

Even when the sun stops shining, and no one
is left to light a candle for the man who hid his poem
in that cellar wall in Berlin, we do not forget
his night where souls assemble, unashamed,
and when the night cannot forget—
I believe in God, he said, *even when God
is silent*—let his scrawl in that cellar
not lie on some dank beach, anonymous,
no scroll; as strike showers come, low waves
seething, let them come, let breath, paper,
black rain, chimneys, Auschwitz; white rain,
Majdanek; let them slice down once, twice,
Belsen, and so forth; then, let night rest.

At Twilight near Agate Bay

We pass a young girl playing
with a yellow toy shovel on her lawn;
I think of my sister who no longer sleeps
with the moon in her box.

At least Chloe has her own place.
When I asked if she remembers
throwing cut grass near Barnstable,
how we laughed, she said, *Don't ask.*

In Hebrew, *holy* means *separate.*
Between one dusk and another,
these birdcalls over wet grass—
the girl builds her separate house.

Baby Evening Grosbeak Caught in Blueberry Netting

All fear and desire—brown wing-beat
after wing-beat—this blur cannot burst
from its prison. You open a chute,
say, *Out!* Dazed angels, we chase

and chasten from one end of our netting
to the next. You untie twisty-ties—
the nestling bites the flesh
between your palm and thumb,

escapes into a blue spruce,
chitters at us sun-struck wardens.
Soon a full-grown songbird,

orange, white, and black, will sprint
from plum tree to hawthorn, cracking
cherry stones in its gold-white beak.

No Palaces, No Bees

—a counselor on 4-South reads his poem to his writing workshop

If you were me, you'd picture the woman on Lakeway,
  a terra cotta warrior, black hair almost lacquered to the side
of her head, and you knew she was one of your people

like that tall man rigid with anaphylactic shock you and your charge
  nurse Dee eased down to the gray carpet by the glowing
    nurses station.
She filled her syringe with Benadryl, gave him the injection

that saved his life, as mine was saved, almost fifty years ago.
  This pen's running out; I ask to borrow our teacher's.
As she ransacks her purse, I think of pocket books

we check for Sharps—no palaces, no bees, lots of mirrors,
  once some weed Dee locked in her med cabinet.
Our teacher doesn't use a special pen, she said,

just this black one. No braided candles like at *Havdallah*
  last evening—*I saw three stars,* said our rabbi. Never thought
I'd go to *shul*, tell you my PSA's are doubling,

round three in this cancer tent; next, female hormones.
  That new patient our doc had me meet in our lobby,
have her sign as a Voluntary patient. *Make sure*

she's talking in her adult voice, not her child voice.
  Better get our teacher a new Rollerball, a twelve pack,
like the ones lined up on Dee's counter.

Will my voice change? Last night's dream,
  how the man in shock threaded his pen
like a geranium through this crevice in his brainpan,

picked up his blue plastic bag of belongings,
  and trudged by me as if toward a strange angel,
as I badged open our locked double doors.

This Wind

Maybe, it's some kind of glitch, the way yellow leaves
   get disembodied, their molecules in the sun. Last week's
storms scattered them, and hard rains swept them down.

As they swirl in eddies over the street, almost a metallic
   sheen. *Eternity, here I come*, said our father
as he hurtled to earth in his dream. The "h" he gave

back to our name—it means *return*, he told us.
   After our mom died, my sister said, *She's up there
with Edith and Paul and everyone.* When this red light

turns green, I pull over by a Midas Muffler,
   scribble *twice in my tide.* Twice in my tide? This wind.
No gold shoals and solstices, no shirring of cloth.

At the end, leaves like this in the sun, in the dust—
   the fastened veins in their sleep?—and we turn.

After Sunup Near the Y Road

I'm thinking of a movie from almost fifty years ago.
The woman asked, *Do you hear the bells?* Someone
replied, *Are you sure?* As if that were an answer.
Out our living-room window now, low fir branches

almost block the light. There's the dusty cylinder
of our bird feeder, the black metal bar bent down—
a gray squirrel hangs from its hind feet. Last night,
our online *seder*. The cantor led this prayer,

Eli, Eli, Lord, Lord. Her windowsills, white walls,
high windows. Her small son slipped in and out
of the room. I've never seen angels up and down

a ladder, never saw Elijah. On my laptop,
her cool white walls. How come no shadows?
Now this gray glass cylinder in the sun.

I remember nothing else about the movie.

Deer in Fog at Twilight near Squalicum Lake Road

Snow flurries more sparse—my sister
no longer sleeps in her cardboard box.
As if to measure me, this brown-tailed deer
has paused by a grove of alders.

She flexes her haunches, ears flicking.
I have nothing to say to the dark, except
why question what light we're given—
the doe almost quiet as water.

Night Journey

The mountains haven't been leveled.
The street is still a street. I pick up your suitcases,
walk with you, no yellow half-moon
low in the sky,

The last brick house
with the oak door, arched elm trees...
Father, you wear your jacket of stars.
Mother, you sing an old song.

Aubade: As We Stand under the Eleventh Street Bridge

—*for Linda*

This bright, pale new grass in the sun.
Gray stanchions almost like pilings
at the bottom of the sea. Last night
you told me, *If I die before you do,
scatter my ashes in the woods
beside some trillium.* You showed
me three white petals pressed
in your book. Now as cars
cross by, the bridge gathers its weight
and starts to break in waves, as one
by one the large boards rise
and shudder.
              What's the matter?
you ask. Like a face in a rearview
mirror, a song I cannot hear—
under the echoing bridge,
these gray stanchions.
A faint haze of green in the air—
yes, our disquiet this April;
almost nothing happens; we wait.
And no, this is not a prayer.

Acknowledgments

The author offers grateful acknowledgment to the editors of the following publications in which these poems first appeared:

The Bridge: "At the Alger Swap Meet"

Califragile: "Aubade: As We Stand under the Eleventh Street Bridge"; "Now The Lion Sun"; and "After Sun-Up Near the Y Road"

Chiron Review: "Before the Party, You Tell Me, I've Got Three Years Left, Maybe Five" and "Almost Every Crevice: A Counselor on 4-South Speaks"

"Missing"; "Did You Ever Call the Cops on Me, Asks My Sister on the Phone"; and "As We Get Ready to Go See Chloe" are forthcoming

Cirque: "Prophet on Railroad Avenue"

Crab Creek Review: "Where the Voices Took Her"; "Looking For My Sister"; "Clarity"; and "This Wind"

Crack The Spine: "As We Drive South through Skagit Valley near Midnight"

Door Is a Jar: "Sidewalks and My Sister"

Grey Sparrow: "Early Sunday Morning during Threats Of War with North Korea"

Jeopardy: "'Devereux'"

Main Street Rag Review: "Wildfires, St. Paul Riots"

Northwind Anthology: "Green's Idea"

Off The Coast: "Baby Evening Grosbeak Caught in Blueberry Netting"

Open: A Journal Of Art And Letters: "When We Send My Sister Birkenstocks, She Gives Them Away"; "Kristallnacht, 1938: Night of Shattered Glass"; "At O'Hare Airport: Her Foxgloves"; and "Deer in Fog at Twilight near Squalicum Lake Road"

Permafrost: "Taking Him Home"

Poetry Superhighway: "Another Shooter" and "Late Afternoon in August: 1970"

Psaltery and Lyre: "Night Journey"

Red Rock Review: "Afterward (2)"

Shot Glass Journal: "At Twilight near Agate Bay" and "The Whale Thank-You Card You Send Me from the Museum of Natural History"

Sue Boynton Contest Winners: "Her Peonies" and "The Possum on Irving Street after Evening Services"

Sweet Tree Review: "In a Lutheran Cemetery in Seattle"

"At the Alger Swap Meet" and "Feeding the Animals" were included in the chapbook *Disappearances* (Radiolarian Press)

"Her Story of Fire"; "Afterward"; "Where the Voices Took Her"; "Looking for My Sister"; and "We've Come to Moclips to Forget" were in the chapbook *Her Story Of Fire* (Egress Studio Press).

Califragile posted "Another Shooter"

Cathexis Northwest Press posted "Taking Him Home"

Open posted "Green's Idea"

The author wishes to thank Gayle Kaune, Patricia Hooper, and Joe Stroud for their close reading of poems, and for their generous support. Thanks also to Linda Conroy, Barbara Bloom, and Jay Nahani-Braunstein. The community of Madrona poets at Fort Wooden also deserves a shout-out: Tom Aslin, Michael and Toni Hanner, Jordan Hartt, Gayle Kaune, Jenifer Lawrence, Karen Seashore, Diana Taylor, and David Thornbrugh. I'm grateful to Centrum for many residencies and to Christine Cote for bringing out this book. Thanks to Ria Harboe for her lovely cover image. Most of all, I want to thank Linda Ford.

About the Author

Richard Widerkehr's work has appeared in *Atlanta Review, Rattle, Writer's Almanac,* and others. He earned his M.A. from Columbia University, won two Hopwood first prizes for poetry at the University of Michigan, first prize for short story at the Pacific Northwest Writers Conference, three Sue C. Boynton Poetry Contest awards, and three awards for poems published in *The Bridge*. He has poems in *Take A Stand: Art Against Hate* (Raven Chronicles Press), which won the 2021 Washington State Book Award for poetry. His other books and chapbooks include *At The Grace Cafe* (Main Street Rag Publishing), *In The Presence Of Absence* (MoonPath Press), *Her Story of Fire* (Egress Studio Press), *The Way Home* (Plain View Press), and a novel, *Sedimental Journey* (Tarragon Books). He has taught writing in the Upward Bound Program at Western Washington University and has worked as a case manager for the mentally ill. He reads poems for *Shark Reef Review*.

Shanti Arts

Nature ▪ Art ▪ Spirit

Please visit us online
to browse our entire book catalog,
including poetry collections and fiction,
books on travel, nature, healing, art,
photography, and more.

Also take a look at our highly regarded art
and literary journal, *Still Point Arts Quarterly*,
which may be downloaded for free.

www.shantiarts.com

www.ingramcontent.com/pod-product-compliance
Lightning Source LLC
LaVergne TN
LVHW041342080426
835512LV00006B/585